PICTURE PROMPTS
Prepositions and Directions

Susan Thomas

Miniflashcards
Language Games

First published 1997

© DELTA Publishing 1997
© Artwork and original text MiniFlashcard Language Games 1996

Typesetting by CjB Editorial Plus

Text and cover design by Darren Watts

Printed and bound in the UK

Project Management: Swan Communication Ltd, England
Adapted Text: Susan Holden

Based on material developed by MiniFlashcard Language Games, PO Box 1526, London W7 1ND

This edition published by DELTA Publishing, 39 Alexandra Road, Addlestone, Surrey KT15 2PQ

ISBN: 1 900783 17 7

Picture Prompts: Prepositions and Directions

CONTENTS

Language Chart

Introduction to *Picture Prompts*

1.1 What *Picture Prompts* contains

Notes

Each *Picture Prompts* book contains:
- a description of ways of using games and game-like activities in foreign language teaching;
- a menu of 20–30 standard activities which can be used with the specific picture cards;
- photocopiable sets of pictures to use around a theme (eg Clothes), or to provide practice in a specific language area (eg Phrasal Verbs or Adjectives);
- instructions for using the pictures, including:
  - vocabulary list;
  - useful language;
  - suitable standard activities;
  - additional activities;
- spinners to photocopy and cut out for use with games;
- blank boards to photocopy and use to make your own games.

Each book thus provides a rich resource of ideas and photocopiable materials which can be used with a wide range of age groups and language levels.

1.2 Using games in the language classroom

Notes

Games and game-like activities provide excellent ways of allowing learners to practise language in a relaxed, creative way. They encourage the repetition of key language items in a way which is motivating and challenging. New lexical items and grammatical structures can be used within familiar game-like formats, thus providing the slower learners with support and guidance, while allowing the faster ones to use their creativity.

The practice provided through *Picture Prompts* extends that contained in the course book, and allows mixed ability classes to work in groups at their own pace.

1.3 Preparing the picture sheets

Notes

The picture sheets can be prepared in different ways:
- They can be photocopied onto paper, for use as handouts or worksheets.
- They can be enlarged, for use as flashcards or posters.
- They can be copied onto card, and cut out, to make individual cards for use in games.
- Text can be added beneath the pictures, or on the back.
- To protect the pictures, they can be copied onto paper, glued onto card, and then covered with acetate.
- They can be photocopied onto acetate to provide OHP transparencies.
- The visuals can be combined or grouped to make display materials, or to make a picture dictionary or topic reference book.
- The blank masters can be used to create new sets of visuals, and to make matching text cards and new games.

1.4 Using the picture sheets

Notes

The visuals can be used to:
- introduce a new word or phrase;
- serve as a prompt for spoken language in a practice or review activity;
- serve as a reminder of the meaning of a written word or phrase;
- provide the starting point for introducing or revising related vocabulary;
- illustrate a structure, often in combination with other pictures;
- provide a series of examples to illustrate a teaching point;
- provide random prompts, when used in conjunction with a spinner or die, for practice or assessment.

1.5 Language presentation

Notes

Introduce new language, using the visuals as flashcards, or on the OHP. Provide plenty of time for the language to be heard and practised before you ask any student to speak alone. Chorus work and class repetition are useful here. Encourage the learners to experiment with their voices: they can repeat the words in different ways, eg emphatically, softly, angrily, questioningly, etc. This helps to avoid boredom, and encourages good intonation and pronunciation.

Learners who are good at relating sounds and visuals will find that they can easily associate language items with the illustrations. Others may find it useful to see the written form as well, so introduction of this should not be delayed. At this stage, attention should be drawn to differences between pronunciation of the written form in English and the students' own language. In this way, these items can be used later as production models by the students.

1.6 Practice activities and games

Notes

Once the learners are familiar with the new vocabulary items, individual or group activities and games can be set up to practise them. Such activities will provide opportunities to practise the items in context, and in association with specific language structures and functions. This will help them transfer the language into their long-term memories.

During the course of an activity, you should help the students with any lexical items or pronunciation features which they are unsure of.

Section 3 (page 9) sets out a collection of standard activity-types which can be used with any of the picture sheets in this book.

The language notes opposite each page of pictures give activities which are designed specifically for that visual set.

1.6.1 Varying the activities

Most of the standard activities are based on well-known games and may be familiar to your class. Younger learners are often very good at making up their own variations, while older ones may rely on you to suggest these. However, adults usually respond well, as they can practise actively without using the language 'in public'.

The important thing is that the learners are practising the language in an active, meaningful way, and are also having fun. Some of the games may generate noise; others are quite quiet. Some are competitive; others require co-operation.

You may wish to decide how to encourage weaker students in the competitive games. These can often be made into exciting team events, using mixed ability teams, with a time element. If this involves physical movement, make sure there are no hazards in the classroom!

For extended practice, you may wish to get the students to move round the room after each game, changing partners and groups. Most games last between 5 and 15 minutes, although the writing activities generally take longer.

Allow time at the end of a game to discuss difficulties, and ideas for varying or improving the game. There may be ways of adapting it to reflect the students' own interests more closely.

1.7 Assessment

1.7.1 Self-assessment

Activities and games based on picture cards are ideal for encouraging the learners to assess their own progress. Once they are sure of particular language items, they can discard these particular cards and use more unfamiliar ones. The cards can be used together later for a test.

1.7.2 Teacher assessment

This can take place:
- during a teacher-controlled activity with the OHP;
- by observing individuals and pairs at work;
- by joining in with groups or individuals during an activity;
- by providing individuals or groups with a worksheet, based on the same visuals.

Such feedback provides information for future reteaching, or for planning future work.

1.8 Grammar practice

Collections of Picture Prompts such as those in the *Adjectives*, and the *Prepositions and Directions* books, can also be used to practise specific grammar patterns, as well as for general communication activities.

1.8.1 Adjectives

The pictures can be used to practise the:
- order of adjectives when more than one is used to describe a noun;
- formation of comparatives and superlatives;
- relationship between adjectives and adverbs.

1.8.2 Prepositions and Directions

The pictures in this book can be used to practise:
- difference in choice of prepositions between L1 and English;
- use of preposition and article.

Using the Pictures

The pictures contained in this book can be used singly, or in a variety of combinations, to support work at different stages of the language programme. They can also be used with students of different abilities, needs and ages.

2.1 Use in class

Notes

The visuals can be used:
- with the whole class, to introduce vocabulary and concepts;
- with individual students and groups, to practise or revise specific language items.

They can be:
- combined in many different ways to illustrate relationships between different areas of vocabulary;
- used in random groups to introduce variety and an element of challenge;
- introduced singly or in groups as the starting point for using language creatively.

Function cards (page 54) can be used in combination with the visuals to encourage the transfer of learning from one context to another.

Board games (page 54) involving the visuals and/or dice and spinners, can be used to set up group activities which are simple or demanding.

2.2 Using the OHP: why

Notes

If available, an OHP is particularly useful for introducing new vocabulary. It can also be used for whole-class work at various stages in the language programme. It can be used to:
- ensure that the students understand the concepts underlying the activity;
- review previously-taught language items before introducing new, associated vocabulary;
- present new language;
- provide teacher-led practice of new language;
- assess whether the new language has been well enough learned for the students to go on to group work activities;
- play whole-class games;
- demonstrate the rules of a game before it is played in groups;
- invite suggestions from the students on ways of using language items in different situations;
- encourage activities which require the students to make creative use of the language they have learned;
- organise feedback on an activity;
- assess learning;
- revise items which were learned earlier in the programme.

2.3 Using the OHP: how

Notes

There are many ways of using the pictures on the OHP. Here are several, which will add variety and interest to your lesson.

- Move the pictures slowly into focus and ask the students to name them.
- Flash the picture up. If it is not named, repeat more slowly.
- Reveal sections of the picture bit by bit.
- Cut the picture into sections, and put on the OHP in random order, and/or upside down. Ask the students to reassemble in the correct order.
- Use as silhouettes.
- Use a keyhole shape cut out of card as a frame. Play 'Through the Keyhole' guessing games.
- Colour the pictures using instructions from the class.
- Add overlays for items such as the price of clothes.
- Use for whole-class games such as *Noughts and Crosses* [3]; *What's on the Card?* [1]; *Kim's Game* [6]; *True or False?*[14]; and *Guessing Game* [13].

Standard Games and Activities

The first group of 18 games and activities described here can be used with any sheet of Picture Prompts in any book of the series, although you may want to vary them slightly. Each is cross-referenced by a number, eg **[1]**, in the individual Lesson Notes.

The second group (page 13) can be used with any sheet of Picture Prompts in this book.

[1]
What's on the Card?   memorising; consolidating

● **Equipment:**   20+ picture cards with text on the back, or a checklist of the text.

a   Picture Spread   **free choice of visible cards**
Spread the cards face up on a table. Take it in turns to pick a card and name it. If you are right, keep the card. If you are wrong, put it back. The player with most cards at the end is the winner.

b   Pick a Card   **free choice of unseen cards**
One player fans out the cards, face down. One player chooses a card and tries to name it. If correct, you keep the card. If incorrect, you put it back, and the cards are shuffled before the next player chooses. The winner is the player with most cards at the end,

c   Take that Card   **no choice of card**
Place the pile of cards on the table, face up. Take it in turns to name the top card, If you are correct, you keep it. If you are incorrect, that card goes to the bottom of the pile. Winner as before.

Variation: If you do not know a card, put it face up on the table in front of you.
It becomes a penalty card. At the end of the game, take it in turns to name these cards. Whoever names the card correctly, wins it.

d   Guess the Card   **choice of unseen cards**
Place a number of cards on the table, face down (no text on back). Take it in turns to choose and name a card. If you are correct: keep it. If you are incorrect: put it back. Winner as before.

e   Quick Flash   **no choice of card; time pressure**
One person holds up a card for one second only. The first player to name it correctly keeps it. Winner as before.

[2]
Line Solitaire   memorising; consolidating; revising

● **Equipment:**   10+ cards per player.

Basic version   **individual learning**
Lay out some cards in a line, face up. Name the first item, and then check with the word on the back. If you get it right, carry on. If you are wrong, learn the word. Then shuffle the cards, lay them out in a new line, and begin again. The winner is the player who completes the longest line.

Variation 1: Put the cards in a diamond or pyramid shape, or in rows of six, and see how many rows you can get right.

Variation 2: Lay the cards in a square 4x4 (you need 16 cards per player). Move from corner to corner in the smallest number of moves.

[3]
Noughts and Crosses   consolidating; revising; monitoring

● **Equipment:**   nine cards.

Basic version

Lay the cards face up in a 3x3 shape. Take it in turns to name them. If you are correct, turn the card over, or put a coloured counter on it. The next player tries to name a card next door to it. Three named cards in a row wins the game.

[4]
Three in a Row   creative use of language

● **Equipment:**   any page of 20 pictures relating to a topic. Three counters for each player.

Basic version

Choose a picture square, and name the item on it, or say something about the picture. If you are right, put a coloured counter on it. The first player with three counters in a row is the winner.

Variation: Use a 20-sided spinner. Proceed as above, but use the spinner to select the squares.

[5]
I Spy ...   consolidating; revising

● **Equipment:**   cards.

Basic version

Put some cards face up on the table. One player calls out the first letter of an item. The first player to point to a correct card beginning with that letter, wins it. That player calls the next letter. The winner is the player with most cards at the end of the game.

[6]
Kim's Game   consolidating; revising

● **Equipment:**   cards.

Basic version

Spread out cards face up on the table. All the players turn away, and one player removes one card. The first player to name the missing card wins a point.

[7]
Bingo   consolidating; revising; listening

● **Equipment:**   a sheet of 20 cards on a picture board for each player.
     Eight counters for each player.

Basic version

Each player chooses eight items from the 20-picture sheet and puts a cross in the corner of each. The quiz person calls out the 20 items in any order. If you have put a cross next to that item, you can put a counter on it. The first player to put a counter on all their marked squares calls 'Bingo!' and is the winner.

Variation 1: The quiz person uses the 20-sided spinner to select the words called.

Variation 2: Spread out 20 cards face up on the table. The quiz person removes them, and you write down ten words you can remember. The quiz person then shuffles the cards, and puts them down one after the other. Check your ten words against these. The first player to have ten words correctly spelled on their list is the winner.

[8]
Charades
consolidating; revising

● **Equipment:** cards.

Basic version
The first player chooses a card and mimes the item for the others to guess.

[9]
Snap
consolidating; revising

● **Equipment:** four sets of cards from the current topic, or previous ones.

Basic version
Shuffle the cards and deal them out. Each player takes it in turn to put a card face up on the table. If two similar cards are put down, the first player to name the cards correctly wins them.

[10]
Dominoes
consolidating; reading

● **Equipment:** sets of dominoes with pictures and text, using the blank square templates (page 56).

Basic version
Distribute six dominoes to each player. Put one domino in the centre of the table. Take it in turns to put your dominoes down, as you match words and pictures.

[11]
Matching Pairs
consolidating; revising

◉ **Equipment:** two sets of picture cards.

Basic version
Shuffle the cards and spread them out face down. The first player turns over two cards. If they are the same, and if you can name them correctly, you can keep them, and have another turn. If they do not match, or if you cannot name them, the cards are put back. It is then the next player's turn.

[12]
I Went to Market
consolidating; revising

● **Equipment:** cards.

Basic version
Spread suitable cards face up on the table. One player says "I went to market, and I bought ...", and adds an item using the cards on the table as a prompt. The next player repeats the sentence and adds another item.

> "I went to the market and I bought (some shoes)."
> "I went to the market and I bought (some shoes) and (a new jacket)."

Any player who gets the sentence wrong, or cannot name a new item, drops out.

[13]
Guessing Game
creative use of language

● **Equipment:** set of cards relating to current topic.

Basic version
The first player thinks of one of the cards and says something about it. The first person to identify the card, wins it.

[14]
True or False?   **listening**

● Equipment: a sheet of cards.

Basic version
One person points to a card, and makes a true or false statement about it. The person who correctly says "True" or "False" wins the card.

Variation 1: As above, but the second player repeats the sentence if it is true, or corrects it if it is false.
Variation 2: One person reads out a list of true or false statements about the pictures. The players make a note of whether each is true or false.

[15]
Battleship Buddies   **speaking; listening**

● Equipment: two identical sets of nine cards for each pair.

Basic version   **pairwork**
Player A puts the cards in a 3x3 shape behind a book, so that Player B cannot see them. Player A describes each card, and says where it is, eg "In the middle of the top row". Player B tries to arrange his/her cards in the same way. Then they compare.

Variation: Draw pictures on the grid, instead of using cards.

[16]
Following Instructions   **listening**

● Equipment: one identical picture for each student.

Basic version
Give instructions to follow, eg:

> "Draw a flower in the middle of the T-shirt. Give it some leaves. Colour the flower red and the T-shirt yellow. Then put a cross at the bottom of the picture. Now draw a line across the top of the picture. Finally, fold the picture into four, and put it in your coursebook between pages 60 and 61."

Ask the students to compare what they have done.

[17]
Spot the Difference   **creative use of language; speaking; listening**

● Equipment: two enlarged copies of a picture for each pair.

Basic version   **pairwork**
Player A changes his/her picture by adding or deleting things. Player B asks questions to find out what the changes are, and makes similar changes. Compare your pictures.

[18]
Storytime   **creative use of language; writing**

● Equipment: mixed cards.

Basic version
Give each player some cards from mixed sets. Each player has 10-15 minutes to write a short story, incorporating the items on these cards. Each person then reads out their story.

Variation 1: One player starts the story as an oral activity. The others take it in turns to add a sentence.

Variation 2: Use the activity for homework, and ask the students to record their stories on a cassette. Play them back in class.

Variation 3: Learners or groups select three or four cards at random. They then make up a story, or act out a scene, using the cards as prompts.

Standard activities which can be used with any sheet of Picture Prompts in this book.

[19]
Twenty Questions

creative use of language; speaking; listening

● Equipment: a sheet showing a place or map.

Basic version

Choose an item from the picture sheet and write it down. Other players can ask you 5–20 questions to discover what you have chosen. They can only ask "yes/no" type questions.

[20]
Following Directions

listening

● Equipment: town plans for each group or individual.

Basic version

Give an itinerary, which the students mark on their own maps.

[21]
You are Here

creative use of language; speaking; listening

● Equipment: a map or plan for each group or pair.
A counter for each player.

Basic version   **pairwork**

Place a counter to show where you are. Now give each other directions to reach another place on the map. Move your counters.

[22]
Shopping List/Treasure Hunt/Family Outing

creative use of language; speaking; listening

● Equipment: a town map.
Six object cards.

Basic version   **pairwork**

Your partner must collect the items on the picture cards. Give instructions to go round the town as quickly as possible to collect them.

[23]
Simon Says

listening

● Equipment: selected cards for each player.

Basic version   **pairwork**

One player gives instructions to move the cards, eg
> "Put your pen on the table. Put the pencil next to the pen. Put the pen under your book ..."

[24]
A Dog's Life

creative use of language; writing

● Equipment: preposition pictures and Spot the Dog visual.

Basic version

Make up a story about a day or hour in the life of a dog. Use some of the pictures to illustrate it.

Key language

Prepositions and Directions 1

1 where's ...?
2 (over) here
3 (over) there
4 near
5 far (from)
6 straight on
7 left
8 right
9 first left
10 second left
11 third right
12 (go) over
13 (go) under
14 (go) through
15 to, towards
16 from
17 in
18 on
19 under
20 in front of

Prepositions and Directions 2

21 behind
22 next to
23 between
24 on either side of
25 against
26 opposite
27 at the end of
28 at the edge of
29 in the middle of
30 at the back of
31 in the corner of
32 on the wall
33 on the floor
34 at the top of
35 at the bottom of
36 upstairs/on the first floor
37 downstairs/on the ground floor
38 outside
39 inside
40 at (my) house

Group A: Direction and Distance

Picture Cards: Vocabulary on cards 1–15; selected items from 16–39.

Useful language

Notes	Where's the ...? Can you tell me where (the) ... is?
	Can you tell me the way to ...?
	Excuse me, I'm looking for ...
	You go ..., then ....
	Is the (post office) near here? How far is the (post office)?
	It's quite near, you can walk to it.
	It's quite far, you'll have to get a bus.

Standard games and activities (see Section 3, pages 9–13)

Notes	[1]	What's on the Card?
	[11]	Matching Pairs
	[14]	True or False?

Prepositions Etc

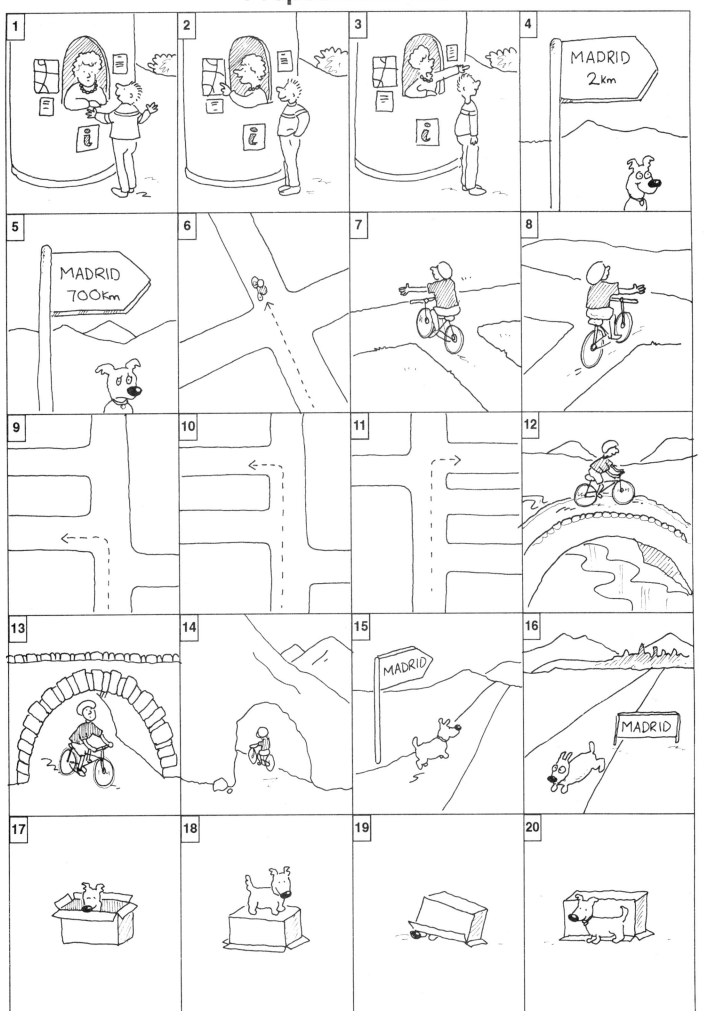

Additional Activities for these picture sheets

Notes

Giving directions

Use the cards together with a map or plan to give directions. Each sentence must use one of the cards, eg

> second left
> "To get to the garage, take the second left after the campsite."

Group B: Location and relative position

Picture Cards: Vocabulary on cards 4, 5, 15–40.

Useful language

Notes

The dog is in the box.   Is the dog in the box?
Is the dog on the box or in it?
Where's the dog?   In the box.
Where are the dogs?   They're ...

Standard games and activities (see Section 3, pages 9–13)

Notes

[1]   What's on the Card?
[13]   Guessing Game
[16]   Following Instructions

Old Town (pages 18 and 19)

Key language

Notes

Appropriate language from page 14.

castle
newsagents/paper shop
theatre

Useful language

Notes

The (bank) is next to the (post office).
Is the (bank) next to the (post office)?   Yes/No.

Excuse me, where's the (bank)?
It's opposite the (post office), next to the (church), between ... and ...
How far is it to the (bank)? Not far, it's (at the end of the street).

Standard games and activities (see Section 3, pages 9–13)

Notes

[13]   Guessing Game
[14]   True or False?
[20]   Following Directions
[22]   Family Outing

Additional Activities for these picture sheets

Notes

A   Finding your way round

Draw maps or plans of other places for similar activities:
airport
art gallery
hospital
museum
island
your town

B   Walking tour

You are a Tour Guide. Write a description of a walking tour of one of the above for a Tourist Brochure.

You could record this on cassette.

Old Town

New Town (pages 20 and 21)

You can use this plan to prompt directions for pedestrians, cyclists or motorists. You can draw in traffic lights, one-way systems and street signs. You can enlarge the plan and write in the street names.

Key language

Notes

Appropriate language from page 14.

park
petrol station
supermarket

Useful language

Notes

Where's the (park), please?   It's ...
Do you know where the (park) is?
Can you tell me the way to ...?

Are you driving? In that case, ...

You'll see the (town hall) on your left. After that, take the (second right) ...

Standard games and activities (see Section 3, pages 9–13)

Notes

[13]   Guessing Game
[14]   True or False?
[20]   Following Directions

Additional Activities for these picture sheets

Notes

A Your school

Draw a plan of your school.
You are taking visitors round it. Explain where things are.

Variation: You are taking a disabled visitor around it.

B Your area

Bring in a map of your local area. Use it for the following activities:

- describing how you get from the train or bus station to your home;
- describing how you get from your home to school;
- writing a suggested route for a carnival procession or a demonstration.

New Town

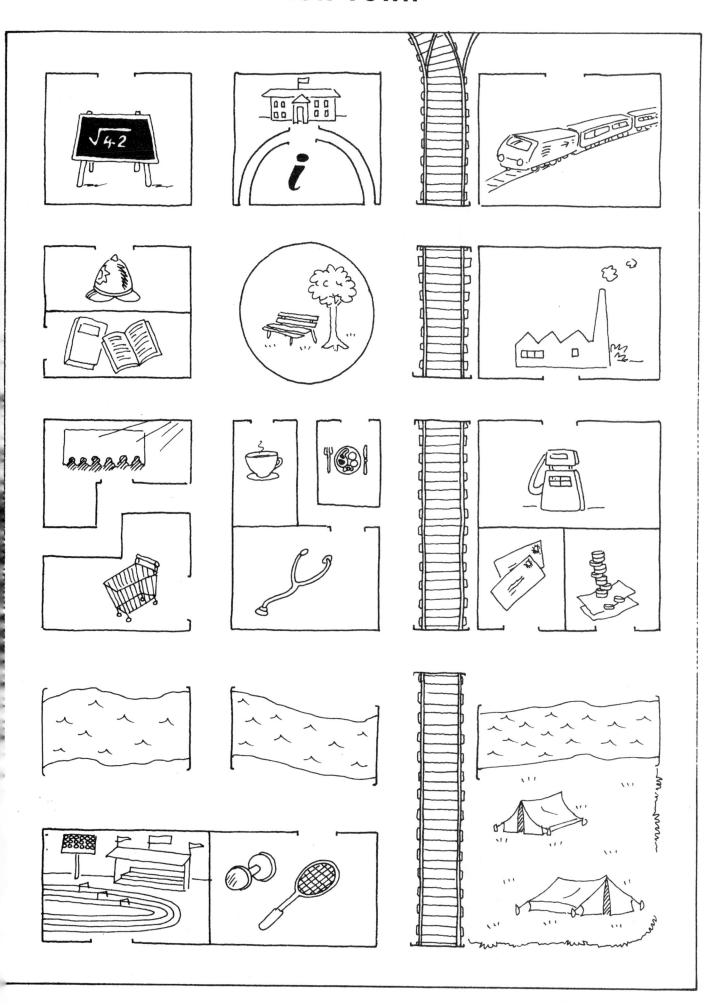

One-way system (pages 22 and 23)

Key language

Notes

Appropriate language from page 14.

park
petrol station
supermarket

Useful language

Notes

Where's the (park), please?   It's ...
Do you know where the (park) is?
Can you tell me the way to ...?

Are you driving? In that case, follow the one-way system until you see ....

Standard games and activities (see Section 3, pages 9–13)

Notes

[20]   Following Directions

One Way System

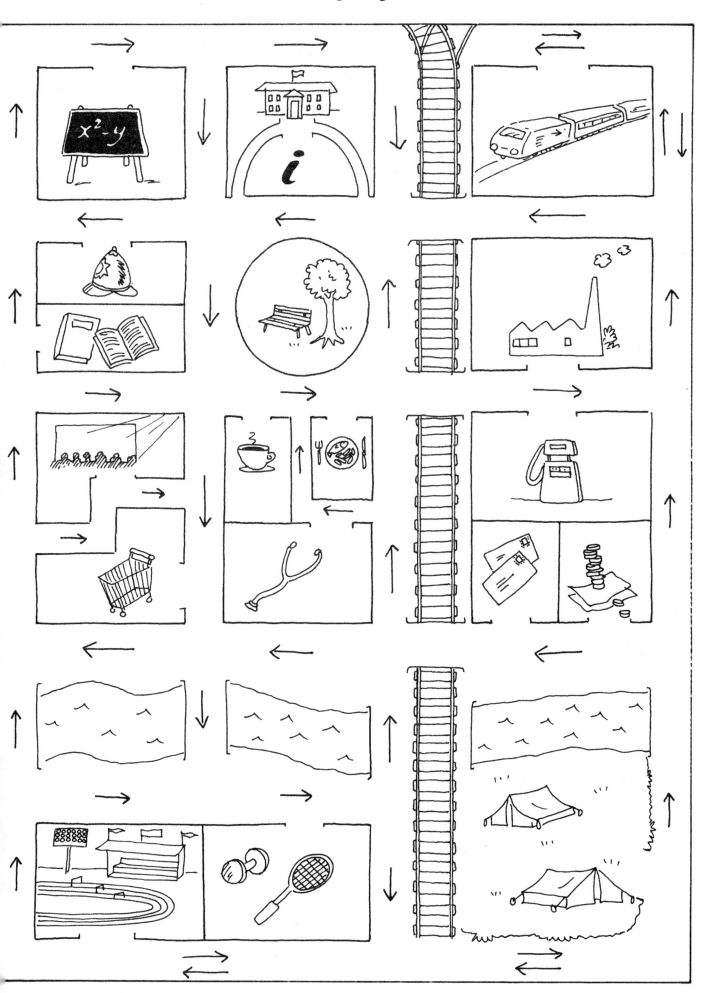

At the Campsite (pages 24 and 25)

Key language

Notes

Appropriate language from page 14.

cafe
launderette
showers

Useful language

Notes

Where's the (swimming pool), please?   It's ...
Do you know where the (swimming pool) is?
Can you tell me the way to (the shop)?

I booked a tent next to the (swimming pool).

Where's the (office)?   Behind (reception).

Standard games and activities (see Section 3, pages 9–13)

Notes

[13]   Guessing Game
[14]   True or False?
[20]   Following Directions

Additional Activities for these picture sheets

Notes

Your ideal campsite

Draw a plan of your ideal campsite.
You are working in the Reception Office. Explain where things are.

Variation: Write a description of it for a travel brochure.

At the Campsite

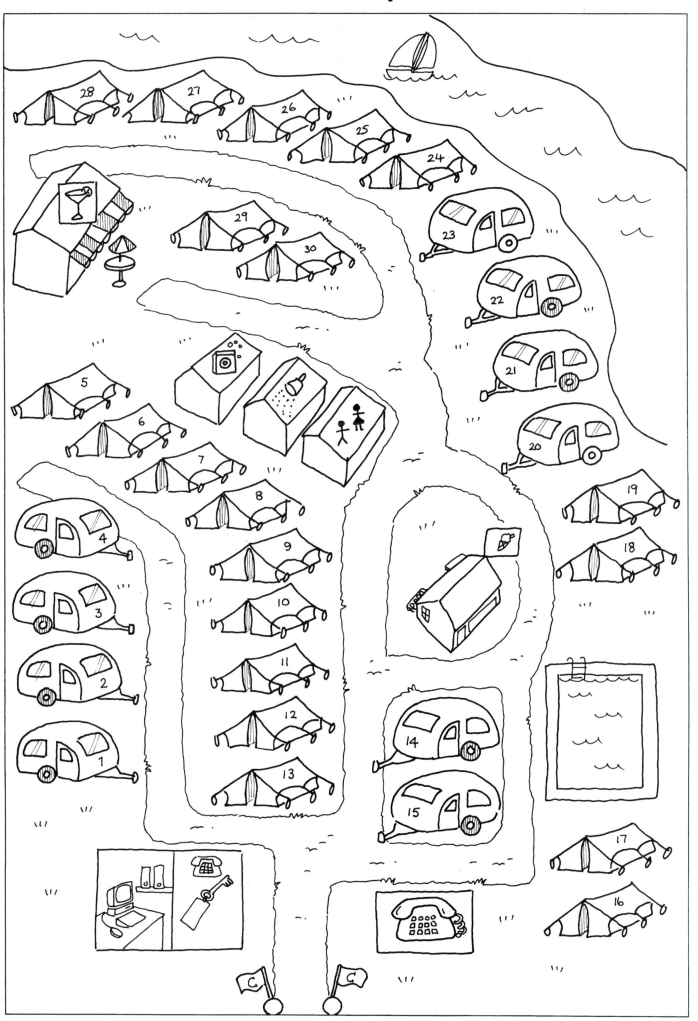

At the Hotel (pages 26 and 27)

Key language

Notes

Appropriate language from page 14.

bedroom
games room
lift
stairs

Useful language

Notes

Where's the (lift), please?   It's ...
Do you know where the (lift) is?
Can you tell me the way to the (lift)?

I booked a room overlooking the (sea). Mine's next to the (car park).
My room is too (noisy).   Is there a (quieter) one?

Standard games and activities (see Section 3, pages 9–13)

Notes

[13]   Guessing Game
[14]   True or False?
[20]   Following Directions

Additional Activities for these picture sheets

Notes

Your ideal hotel

Draw a plan of your ideal hotel, or a real one which you know.
You are working in the Reception Office. Explain where things are.

Variation: Write a description of the hotel for a travel brochure.

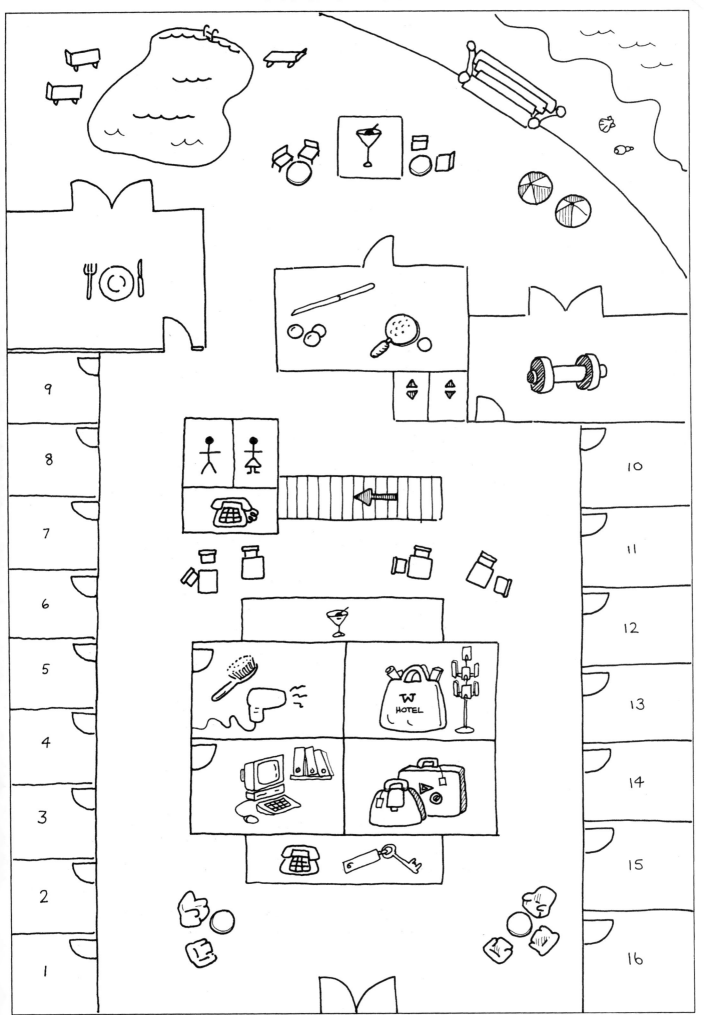

At the Superstore (pages 28 and 29)

Key language

Notes

Appropriate language from page 14.

baked beans
blouses
cat and dog food
milk
spoons

Useful language

Notes

Where's (sugar), please?   It's over there, next to (rice).
Can you tell me where the (yoghurt) is?

Go down there and turn (right) at the end, after the (vegetables).

Standard games and activities (see Section 3, pages 9–13)

Notes

[13]   Guessing Game
[14]   True or False?
[15]   Battleship Buddies
[20]   Following Directions
[22]   Shopping List

Additional Activities for these picture sheets

Notes

Use a blank piece of paper to draw similar plans for:
- a small shop;
- place settings at table;
- kitchen cupboards.

At the Superstore

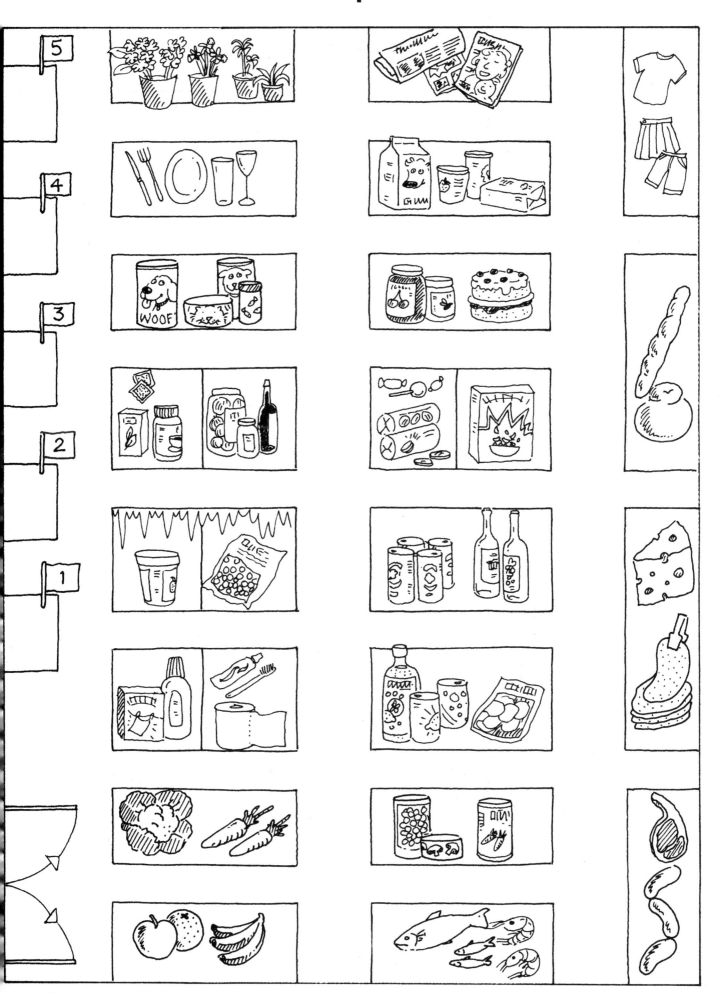

At the Careers Convention (pages 30 and 31)

A careers convention is often held in a school. People come from outside to tell the students about the jobs they may do, and the training they will need.

Key language

Notes

Appropriate language from page 14.

Useful language

Notes

What do you want to be?   A (policeman).
Over there, next to the (customs officers).

Where's the (doctor's) stand?

Where can I find Stand (13)?   Opposite Stand (15).

Standard games and activities (see Section 3, pages 9–13)

Notes

[13]   Guessing Game
[14]   True or False?
[20]   Following Directions

Careers Convention

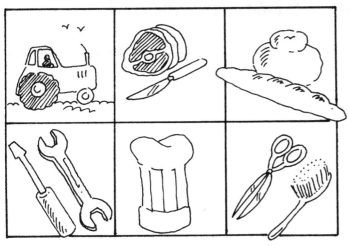

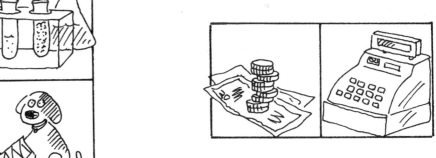

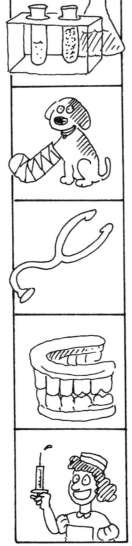

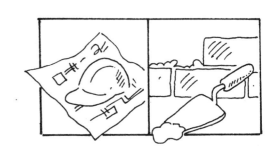

What's Where? (pages 32 and 33)

Key language

Notes

The visual illustrates some common prepositions:

behind
in
in front of
next to
on
under

1 The cat's on the chair.
2 The pig's behind the tree.
3 The mouse is in front of the box/packet.
4 The spider's on the matchbox.
5 The spider's in the matchbox.
6 The dog's in the basket.
7 The pig's in the tree.
8 The cat's behind the chair.
9 The pig's next to the tree.
10 The chicken's under the table.

11 The spider's next to the matchbox.
12 The bird's on the (bird) table.
13 The bird's in the cage.
14 The pig's in front of the tree.
15 The cat's under the chair.
16 The dog's next to the basket.
17 The cat's next to the chair.
18 The mouse is behind the box/packet.
19 The spider's under the matchbox.
20 The cat's in front of the chair.

Standard games and activities (see Section 3, pages 9–13)

Notes

[11]   Matching Pairs
[13]   Guessing Game
[14]   True or False?

Additional Activities for these picture sheets

Notes

Give and receive instructions

Work in groups and give instructions to draw similar simple pictures. Compare the results.

What's Where ?

What's Wrong? (pages 34 and 35)

Key language

1 The plant's under the table.
2 The cup's under the saucer.
3 The TV's under the table.
4 The flowers are under the vase.
5 The armchair's behind the TV.
6 The sunshade's in the pool.

7 The dog's under the basket.
8 The goalkeeper's beside the goal.
9 The teacher's behind the board.
10 The toilet roll's in the toilet.
11 The monitor's in front of the keyboard.
12 The caravan's in front of the car.

Useful language

Notes

Say what's wrong.

The (plant) is under the (table). It should be on the (table).
Put the (TV) on the (table).

Standard games and activities (see Section 3, pages 9–13)

Notes

[4]   Three in a Row
[13] Guessing Game
[14] True or False?

What's Wrong ?

Arranging a Room (pages 36 to 38)

Key language

1	next to	6	on the right (of)
2	in front of	7	on the left (of)
3	behind	8	in the middle (of)
4	between	9	at the front
5	near		

Notes	armchair
	fireplace
	rug

Standard games and activities (see Section 3, pages 9–13)

Notes	[6] Kim's Game

Additional Activities for these picture sheets

Notes

A Information gap 1   Listening

The teacher arranges objects in the room, and then describes the room. The pupils try to do the same.

B Information gap 2   Pairwork

As above. Compare your rooms.

C Information gap 3   Pairwork

The students in each pair have the objects in different positions. They must ask and answer questions to find the difference.

D Moving house

Write instructions for the furniture removers to put the furniture in the room.

Arranging a Room (1)

Arranging a Room (2)

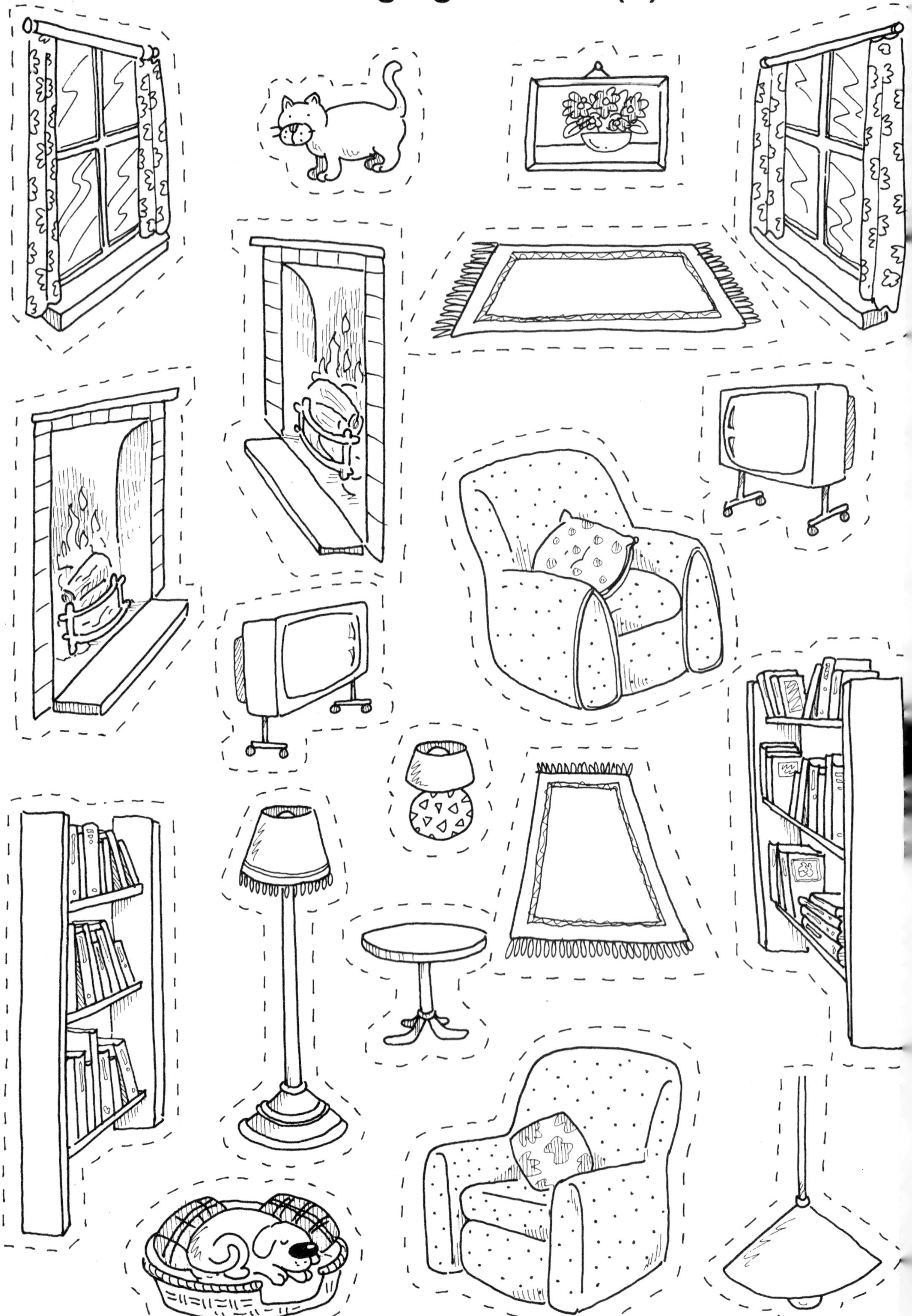

Spot the Dog (pages 39 to 41)

Key language

Vocabulary from page 14 with these numbers:

17 in	**21** behind	**28** at the edge of
18 on	**22** next to	**29** in the middle of
19 under	**23** between	**32** on the wall
20 in front of	**24** on either side of	**31** in the corner of
		38 outside

These prepositions can be applied to the dogs in Picture A (page 40).

Useful language

Notes	
	Dog 1 is in the corner. Is Dog 1 in the corner? Where's Dog 1? In the corner.

Standard games and activities (see Section 3, pages 9–13)

Notes	
	[6] Kim's Game
	[13] Guessing Game
	[14] True or False?
	[17] Spot the Difference
	[19] Twenty Questions
	[24] A Dog's Life

Spot the Dog (1)

Spot the Dog (2)

On the Football Pitch (pages 42 and 43)

Key language

Notes

at the back of	in the middle of
at the edge of	next to
behind	on either side of
between	on the left of
in front of	on the right of
inside	opposite
in the corner of	outside (the field/goal area)

centre forward
goal keeper
left forward

Useful language

Notes

Player No 9 is (opposite) Player No 5.

Standard games and activities (see Section 3, pages 9–13)

Notes

[6]   Kim's Game
[13]   Guessing Game
[14]   True or False?
[15]   Battleship Buddies
[17]   Spot the Difference
[19]   Twenty Questions

Football Pitch

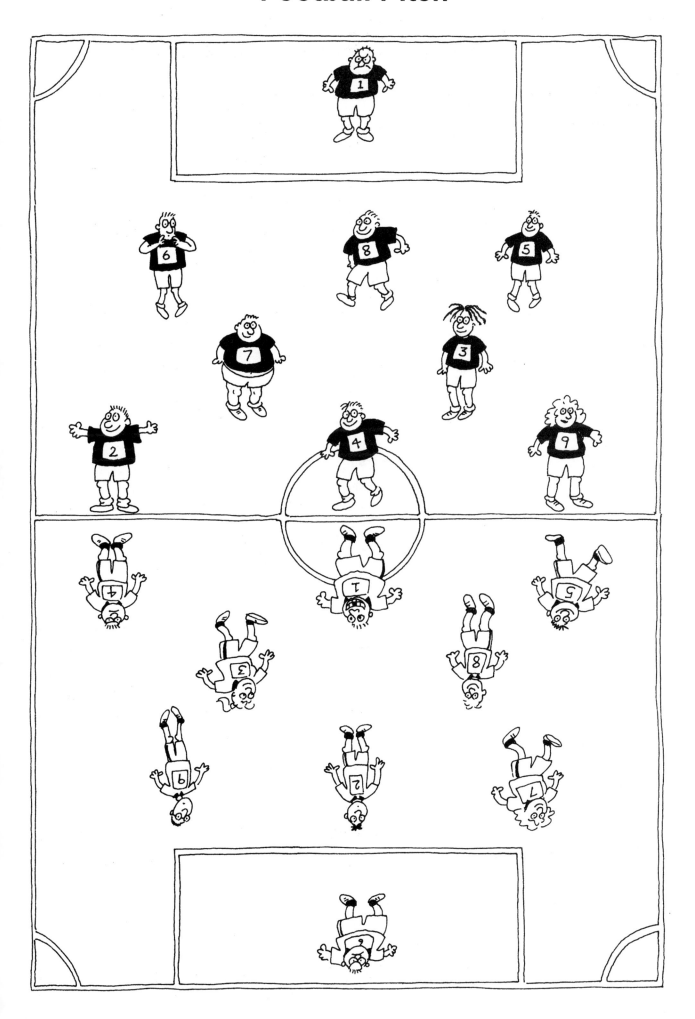

Who Lives Where? (pages 44 to 47)

Key language

Notes

above
below
first floor
ground floor
next to
opposite
under

Standard games and activities (see Section 3, pages 9–13)

Notes

[6]   Kim's Game
[13]   Guessing Game
[14]   True or False?
[15]   Battleship Buddies
[17]   Spot the Difference
[19]   Twenty Questions

Additional Activities for these picture sheets

Notes

A   Noisy neighbours

Think of 'difficult neighbours':
- elderly person
- family with teenage children
- journalist
- medical student
- person in wheelchair
- person with dog
- rock musician
- writer

Work in a group and decide where they should live.

B   Who lives where?

Photocopy and cut up the set of preposition cards (page 46). Add your own prepositions in the blank squares.

Use these to help you describe who lives in each flat.

Who Lives Where ?

Who Lives Where ? (2)

on the left	on the right	in the middle	on the ground floor	on the top floor
between	next to	behind	in front of	opposite
below	above	near to	far from	

In the Fridge (pages 48 and 49)

Key language

Notes

at the back of
behind
between
in front of
in the corner of
in the middle of

next to
on the left of
on the right of
on the second/third shelf down
on the top/bottom shelf

Useful language

Notes

Where's the (ham)?   It's on the ...
The (vegetables) are at the bottom.

Standard games and activities (see Section 3, pages 9–13)

Notes

[13]   Guessing Game
[14]   True or False?
[17]   Spot the Difference
[19]   Twenty Questions

Additional Activities for these picture sheets

Notes

Where does this go?   Pairwork

Give your partner instructions to put the food in the fridge.

In the Fridge

In the Wardrobe (pages 50 and 51)

Key language

Notes

at the back of
behind
between
in the corner
in the drawer
next to

on the left of
on the right of
on the top/bottom shelf
underneath

Useful language

Notes

Where's the (hat)?   It's on the ...
The (shoes) are at the bottom, next to the ....

Standard games and activities (see Section 3, pages 9–13)

Notes

[13]   Guessing Game
[14]   True or False?
[17]   Spot the Difference
[19]   Twenty Questions

In the Wardrobe

In the Cupboard (pages 52 and 53)

Key language

Notes

above
at the top/bottom
below
in between

cassette
exercise book
ruler

next to
on the (left) of
on the top/bottom row

Useful language

Notes

The (scissors) are on the second row, between the (paint brush) and the (envelope).
The (key)'s at the bottom on the left, next to the (cassette recorder).

Standard games and activities (see Section 3, pages 9–13)

Notes

[4]   Three in a Row
[13]   Guessing Game
[14]   True or False?
[15]   Battleship Buddies

In the Cupboard

Individualising the materials

Depending on the age and level of your students, you may wish to adapt the basic cards, or to use them in different ways.

4.1 Function cards

Notes

You may want to prepare some written function cards to use in connection with the picture cards. Prepare sets saying such things as:

ASK FOR INFORMATION

COMPLAIN ABOUT SOMETHING

EXPRESS A WORRY

4.2 Make your own games

Notes

The blank masters on pages 55–56 can be used to prepare your own games. These consist of:
- 12-square board;
- 20-square board.

1

2

3

4

5

6

7

8

9

10

11

12

1

2

3

4

5

6

7

8

9

10

11

12

13

14

15

16

17

18

19

20